Thoughts into Words

BJ NORTH

BALBOA.
PRESS

A DIVISION OF HAY HOUSE

Balboa Press books may be ordered through booksellers or by contacting:

Balboa Press
A Division of Hay House
1663 Liberty Drive
Bloomington, IN 47403
www.balboapress.com.au
1 (877) 407-4847

Because of the dynamic nature of the Internet, any web addresses or links contained in this book may have changed since publication and may no longer be valid. The views expressed in this work are solely those of the author and do not necessarily reflect the views of the publisher, and the publisher hereby disclaims any responsibility for them.

The author of this book does not dispense medical advice or prescribe the use of any technique as a form of treatment for physical, emotional, or medical problems without the advice of a physician, either directly or indirectly. The intent of the author is only to offer information of a general nature to help you in your quest for emotional and spiritual well-being. In the event you use any of the information in this book for yourself, which is your constitutional right, the author and the publisher assume no responsibility for your actions.

Any people depicted in stock imagery provided by Getty Images are models, and such images are being used for illustrative purposes only. Certain stock imagery © Getty Images.

Print information available on the last page.

ISBN: 978-1-5043-1729-0 (sc)
ISBN: 978-1-5043-1730-6 (e)

Balboa Press rev. date: 03/21/2019

Contents

Rock Flower

Amongst the rocks a tiny plant grew.
It struggled against odds,
no good soil, not much water,
no tender care from a gardener,
but it still battled on.

Then a little girl saw it there,
took an interest in watching it struggle.
She sometimes scooped a handful of water
the drops drying on the rocks,
but some landing near the roots
and sucked greedily by the plant.

Weeks went by with the girl watching and waiting.
The plant grew forming a bud on a slender stalk,
day after day she waited to see it bloom.
The day came at last for the blossom to open,
the little girl crouched low to see
a tiny flower in shades of pretty pink
but with a most awful stink.

Rain

This wretched rain,
Here it is again.
Dreary, wet, foggy days
Not even the kids go out to play.

The cold and damp do not inspire
Instead I long for a glowing fire.
Here it is again,
That wretched, rain.

Winter will soon be in the past,
Spring will be here at last.
All the gardens abloom with flowers,
There will be longer daylight hours.

Farmers busy with cows, hay and crops
No time to relax, or looking in the shops.
Gathering up the fruit so ripe and sweet
Swimming, flies, and BBQ meats.

Hot sun, blue sky, clouds way up high,
The green grass going brown and dry.
Then again the cry, rain, rain
Where, is that wretched rain?

I Won, I Won

I won, I won, I bought a ticket and I won!
I was in a rush that day,
Two ladies selling tickets on a cold winter's day,
I just gave them the money and my name,
Then rushed on to get my shopping done,
I never gave it another thought,
Until they rang today, saying "come collect your prize".

I set out ten minutes later in my best outfit,
I arrived in high hopes of a real treat.
The ladies handed me a gift wrapped box,
Too eager to wait I gleefully tore it open,
Only to find carefully wrapped in the box
A Barbie doll, I almost dropped the box in shock,
A Barbie doll and a used one at that.

The ladies smiled and said to me
'The Barbie was a treasured possession of the little girl
We are raising money for who had a nasty accident
She will need a motorised wheel chair.
Her spine was damaged, and she will need constant care,
But her smile makes it all worth while,
So you see you won a real treasure'.

I went and sat in my car, all dressed up and cried.
I was so selfish wanting to have a good time,
While a little girl is facing a challenging change of life.
I will make time today to go and visit
The little girl who gave the only treasure she had
To make her feel worth while from the money raised
To get her the chair so she can move about,
She needs love, help and lots of praise.

Sometimes we buzz through life
never stopping to think of others plight
only thinking of today and the jobs to be done
Forgetting others may be sick or alone
just needing a smile or a kind word or two.

Beneath the Marble

Beneath the marble slab you lie,
Alone in your cold pine box,
All your suffering finally went away.
Around you it is all still and quiet
Except for the seagulls that squawk over the bay
And the soft whisper of the trees in the breeze.

We never had a chance to say goodbye
And slowly time has washed my tears away,
When I am stressed you are here at my side.
I can see the glint of your green eyes
And the slow twitch of your lips before the smile.

What a sad time it would have been,
Without these memories I still have with me.
At times I think you are here walking at my side,
Slowing me when I would have walked on
Not seeing some thing beautiful nor heard our tune
We are still together although far apart.

My Mother

My mother, she was no beauty
her hair was straight, her nose a bit long
She was short and on the chubby side.

But she was always there to wipe a tear,
to listen to our worries and troubles
and give good advice, needed or not.

She lived in a time when affection wasn't shown,
so no cuddles or bedtime stories
but we knew she worried and cared.

Her education was limited, school over at age14
her dreams weren't for big house or money
she just wanted a warm and happy home.

She may not have topped her class
but she made all decisions big and small
with a sense of fairness for all.

She sewed our clothes and knitted jumpers, mended socks
bottled the fruit in season, digging up a veggie plot
to help with the food demands of four growing kids.
Many times over the years she must have worried,
we knew and understood Mum would handle it,
tomorrow was a new day, and all would be ok.

She may have left this earth many years ago now
but her values and thoughts on life
still linger with us all today.

No Goodbye

Whirling, swirling memories and thoughts,
pushing me down into a dark void,
cold, so cold, chilled to the bone.
This is not where I want to be.

Down, down, further down,
shivering, shaking, fingers all numb,
but a strange hot rage is burning deep inside,
then suddenly a noise filters through.

Far away and low, but persistent still,
not the phone or a door bell,
but the cries of a child.
Trembling from head to toe,
I shake myself, wriggle my cold fingers.

Today I roused from the gloom.
But I worry day after day,
if I will always be able to push aside
the inner turmoil to survive another week.

You walked past today and asked if I was ok,
I smiled and nodded.
You didn't see the smile was not real,
its just a mask to hide behind.

Help is there, I am aware,
but what most don't understand,
the tormented soul wont ask for help.
The void is too wide, the pain too deep.

I am used to hiding the unhappiness that rages inside me.
A pain free end I see, is waiting not too far away.
Those left behind will never fully understand
the anguish deep inside me, I just desire peace.

NOTE,... This was written after hearing about a 14yr old girl and
her suicide from bullying

Remember December

Oh, I remember December,
But was it the month I met you, my love
Was it when we wed so long ago?
Was it the month our baby was born?
Was it when you came home with no job?
Was it the month the our little girl left home?
Why do I remember December?

Oh yes, I remember December but why?
Was it the month the house flooded?
Was it the month I crashed the car?
The month my best friend died?
Oh! I remember December..
But why, do I remember December?

Oh why, can't I remember why I remember December?
Was it the month you said goodbye?
Oh I remember December…
But why do I remember December?
Why can't I remember dates in December?
Why do I just remember December…

The Old Farmer

He sat there with the tears streaming down his weathered cheeks,
his shoulders shaking, the sobs coming from deep within.
To see this tough old timer so heart broken was hard.
He had left his wife to cope alone, and went to war as others had done,
he had come through those dreadful years almost un –scathed,
some were badly wounded, many never returned home.

He had struggled on the land year after year,
loosing stock and crops in dreadful droughts,
he had watched the flood waters wash away his soil.
He had lost his wife when they were both still young,
the children they had both wanted had never arrived,
time and years had then crawled along.

He was stooped and his hands now scared and twisted,
he put his wrinkled hand out to pat Old Red,
only have it fall away back down to his leg.
The tears fell again, in those tear filled eyes he saw his dog,
heard his low bark, he felt the soft fur brush against his arm,
he felt the loving lick of Old Red's tongue.

Old Red had walked the fields beside him since a pup,
but now there was no dog, soon there would be no farm.
He slowly stopped crying, closed his eyes and waited
for the dreams to bring his loved ones close to him again.
They may take his farm to pay un-paid bills
but they could never take his memories away.

The Man

The old man with the bulbous nose
ignores people wherever he goes.
He kicks at stones with his big feet,
uncaring about whom he may meet.

On and on he stomps and mutters,
always searching in the gutters.
Clothes now torn with tatters
no one cares about him, it no longer matters.

Once he had a job in the mine,
and lived on good food and a glass of wine.
Then he lost the only one who cared
and with who is life he shared.

A little stray dog she may have been,
but their friendship was a joy to be seen.
Each day at shifts end,
she would be waiting at the gate for her friend.

On days when he was home,
over the hills close by they would roam.
Ten years have passed since the day she died,
now he has no-one to walk at his side,
so on and on he stomps and mutters,
kicking stones and tins in the gutters.

These Special Few

Throughout our lives we choose a special few
To hold close to our hearts
To share impossible dreams
To share the happy times
To help us with the burden of sorrow.
These special few are in our thoughts even when far away
They are there to walk with us on our journey in life.
These special few are special because they too
Share our thoughts and return our love.
They hold us close for comfort
Cherishing us through the good and bad
Helping us to be happy instead of sad.
These special few are the reason we learn
To balance our life in those times of strife.
They may be rich or poor, in health, wealth or wisdom
They may not have had the same choices in life
They be of different colour, country or race
These special few are just forever special to me.

The Man Next Door

The man next door is short and stout,
He perves on me when his wife's not about.
He is as ugly as sin, with long whiskers on his chin.
He is so lazy it drives me crazy,
Watching his wife rush to and fro,
Even the lawn she has to mow.

Sometimes she says "hello" from her door,
But I never wait to hear any more.
Inside I go in a rush,
In case He too comes, to gloat and gush.
I turn the T.V on flop in my comfy chair,
And give lots of cuddles to my old bear.
Relieved that one more time, I got through the firing line.

My friend's advice is outside to stay,
And tell both my neighbors that I'm Gay.
They don't know what the sleazes reaction would be,
I know it would make him sneer in glee.
It would make him try harder even than before,
I may have to punch him on the jaw.
No, I'll shut my mouth, and bide my time,
Till I hang out my Kung-Fu sign.

The Tree

The tree stood alone, aloof, majestic
it was just starting to loose its leaves.
These fluttered silently ground wards
forming a thick carpet of autumn tones.
Lightly thrown together now, but with
Winter rains these would compact and rot,
thus returning vital nutrients back to the tree.
An endless chain.

Below ground the roots had sunk travelling
deep and wide, drawing, compacting the earth.
A warren of large thick shoots,
from which sprung tiny feathery veins.
These sucked, draining any moisture that seeped
sending it slowly upwards,
towards the giant trunk.

Bark, thick and pitted, protected and enamoured
cooling, stabilising the inner life within.
The huge girth that had with stood fierce winds
and burning rays was now casting long shadows.
Secret, cool hiding places, for animals or me
to stand to see, but not be seen.

High up the trunk forked, sending out sturdy limbs
from which spiked smaller branches.
These moved about in the breeze, restless
searching, seeking but also giving.

The branches had stopped their sky ward race
towards the sun and the clean, clear air.
The slight breeze fanned the leaves

parting them to reveal a hidden treasure,
So far above the earth.
A carefully woven nest, of twigs and straw
possibly empty now, but had been home
to a family of tiny birds, protecting them until,
somehow they knew it was time
to leave, to fly away. I knew not where
maybe they will return some day, to this old tree.

When

When my time has come and gone
Maybe I had a chance to say
All those words I wanted to —
But never found the time or right moment
Maybe I never had the chance to hold you again,
Maybe we are never meant to say goodbye.

When your days work has been done
Relax and spare a thought or two
And remember the good times we had
Then smile a while till the memory fades.

File the bad times far away
They are no longer needed,
they will just get in the way
Enjoy each and every day as if your last
Never dwell too long on the unhappy past.

When the sun peeps out from a dark cloud
When the stars glitter so brightly far above
When you feel a gentle breeze in your hair
These are the times I hope you find,
You can feel the love I left behind.

Where Were You

Where were you when I needed you
some one to talk to
to wipe away my tears
to dispel my fears
to gently hold my hand.

When I needed you, where were you?
When I fell and couldn't stand
when my cupboard was empty,
when my Dr rang with bad news
when hope seemed to fade.

Where were you when I needed you?
Where were you?
I needed someone to make me smile
to stay and chat awhile
to talk about memories
and fun in the years gone by

Where are you now my world has crashed
and I have a time limit
that is coming closer by the minute.
Where were you when I needed you?
I need nothing more now
Soon I will be just a memory from your past.

Molly

Battered and broken Molly lay
lightly cushioned and hidden
by fallen autumn leaves.
Her frock of pale blue spun silk
was now a molten, muddy hue.
Her tiny feet had lost one shiny black shoe
one arm protruded at a grotesque angle
from torn silk and leaves.
Her once beautiful face, now scratched, beaten
lifeless, no longer comforting and serene.

Not far away voices of children could be heard
gaily laughing and calling
so happy in the games they played.
Time; for a while forgotten,
as they merrily skipped, jumped and ran
from one swing or slide to another.
Some were throwing a ball skywards so high
then catching it before it bounced to earth.

But the silent sneaking dusk was turning to darkness,
suddenly, all at play stopped and raced for home.
Soon the park was quiet and motionless,
eerie shadows were lurking through bare branches
and sturdy tree trunks.
In the gathering cold darkness Molly still lay
forgotten, in the homewards rush.

Once loved but now no longer needed, it seemed
she would no longer be held in tender hugs
and nor hear any more girlish secrets and dreams.
Molly was now just a broken, discarded doll
thrown away in a thoughtless, childish whim.

Boss-man Jack

Although big in heart body and soul
affection was rarely given and never asked for;
nor a kind word did he speak.
Patience with people was not his virtue
especially when dealing with fools,
at times his bark was worse than his bite.
Others company he did not seek
but they came to him... Boss-man Jack.

He often misunderstood the spoken word,
because his mind was flitting to and fro
from the completion of the last job tackled
to the solution for the new.
Determination to get the job done drove him
to the edge and back at times.
Once started a course of action he plodded on till done
his insight was an impregnable force;
no-one ever questioned the man called Boss-man Jack.

Through life he had plodded with his physical difficulties
now the ticking hands of time were taking their toll.
His once lanky frame was becoming stooped and bent,
his crippled leg dragged a little more each day,
his strong brown hands were losing their grip.
Riches would never come his way;
he was happy just to receive hot food,
or a warm dry place to stay in lieu of pay.
This was ..Boss-man Jack.

'Bye friend

With much sadness I have to say farewell to a close friend
Every morning she waited for me
In times of trouble and stress she was there
I held her in my hand and felt the warmth.

One slip this morning after a very bad night
My hands were trembling and wouldn't still
Clumsily I banged my friend against the tap
I felt the hard contact in my shaky hand.

Now I am sad to say my beloved mug is no more
She is cracked from top to bottom
Although she still looks calm and sweet
She leaked hot coffee all over the bench.

For five years she served me well
my mug didn't deserve this untimely end
carefully I placed her high on the shelf
where I could see her each morning.

Freedom

An eagle drifting and gliding in the air currents above
silently searching below for prey
A flower bud slowly shedding its outer layer
before bursting into a beautiful display
A cocoon of spun threads hides a grub
as it turns into a butterfly, breaks free and flutters away.

A volcano standing high erupts with a burp and rumble
sending hot ash and molten lava into fields below
A tiny rivulet runs gently over stones, merging into a stream
then becomes lost in a mighty river flowing to the sea
Huge dark clouds, merging with a thunderous bang
before releasing hail or huge rain drops to the earth below.

The chip, chip of a beak as it makes a crack the egg shell
finally a fluffy yellow chicken peeps out from inside…..
Tiny turtles break free from the egg nest in the sand
to make a slow dash across the sands for the sea and turning tide
A fly wriggling in a spider web, loosing a wing tangled in the
silken strands
yet still struggles to escape the spider inside….

A mother with a bruised face and tears on her cheeks
prays silently for the pain and problems to cease
A man bent from the shackles, shuffling on cold cement floor
now wishing he had never committed any crime
An un-attended pot bubbling over the top and gurgling onto the
stove
A small child suffering lots of pain as the tiny tooth escapes the
layers of gum.

The relief of kicking off shoes that don't fit
The relief when your bones no longer ache and you are free
A tortured soul finally breaks free from the ties that bind
The freedom to buy what you want, not just what you need
Freedom has different meanings to different situations and people
It can be a state of mind or an actual fact.

Mothering

The baby suckled the breast
while the mother
watched him
and waited
for him to finish,
all the time remembering
and thinking
about all the work
she had to do
and of all the sleep
she had missed out on
since the child
had come into her life,
but knowing too
that she wouldn't
change a thing
about her life
or the baby
or in fact
anything at all.

Fathering

He watched his child

greedily suckle the breast,

and wondered

how he can teach

something so small

to fish, to swim,

hit a ball,

climb a mountain high,

play rough football.

He sighed and turned away.

ANNIE-MAY

She sat in the rocking chair gently rocking to and fro
Her almost sightless eyes stared out the open door.
She did not see the unkempt lawns nor the broken hinged gate.
In her minds eye she saw her son in the different stages of his life,
As a toddler so small, as a teenager so smart at school and sport.
She remembered the day he had left to see the world,
To explore far and wide and to make his fortune.
At first he had sent cards from distant shores,
But as the years passed they had trickled to a stop.

She thought of her husband and his handsome grin,
Smiling as she recalled the good times they had shared.
The fun, laughter, hard work, their closeness and love.
Her crippled fingers twitched as she remembered his last years,
The terrible injuries he had received in a freak accident,
The helplessness of not being able to share the burden of his pain.
The slow agonising years of his suffering,
Then the empty, hollow years that followed.

Annie-May turned her tired eyes inward to the room,
She saw the brightly painted yellow kitchen,
The frilly lace curtains, the jug of flowers on the wooden table.
She licked her lips as she thought of the Sunday roasts,
The bread and cakes she had loved to bake.

The same curtains still hung, although now grey and tattered,
The table now scratched and dusty,
the earthen-ware jug stood cracked and empty.
Cobwebs decorated the peeling yellow paint,
The room smelt damp and musty.

Annie-May sat rocking gently and waiting,

For the son who for years had never returned,
Nor had he sent a loving word.
The rocking chair made soft whispering sounds on the board floor,
Then the gentle rocking slowly ceased;
Annie-May would wait no more.

Head banging

I have tried to explain what was needed,
time and time again I tried, I used different words.
I spoke soft and slow,
I spoke loud, with hand actions.
I yelled the same words.. still no understanding.

I was sore in the throat,
my brain was bouncing around in my skull.
Heaven help me, I prayed silently,
with my eyes squeezed shut,
hoping for a solution to the my dilemma.

Over the years I have had my ears tested,
and been to a speech therapist,
I even went to visit a shrink.
My sanity was intact I was told,
maybe I just needed a holiday,
or not to worry so much nor work so hard.

I am tired and worn out and the day just begun.
I tried again jumbling all the words,
it sounded so ridiculous,
but there it was a smile, a light in his eyes,
He understood.
Heavens Martha, why didn't you just say
that in the first place.

My man though, he wouldn't go,
to get his ears tested, his brain scanned.
He was fine he would say,
I have no problem it is just you.
You need to think before you talk,

get the words in the right order,
then tell me what your problem is.

I have no problem, it is just you,
you have no problem, just me,
the problem, is just me and you..
Or is it you and me?

IF

The old lady looked at the pile of things on the floor
Twenty years had passed, this little heap was all
She had to show, for the time spent on Death Row.
She knelt to the floor to run her fingers over the cover of the books,
To read once again their titles and to open to a favourite page,
To scan the closely typed words that offered salvation from all her sins.
The words should have given her hope, but instead they just added to the pain.
Nor had they helped in coping with the horror within these bleak walls.

All these years and she still knew as she did back at the start,
Nobody dies from a broken heart.
These cold grey bricks and strong steel bars had been her home for so long
Yet she had never made a fuss as some,
Nor made a friend, who her passing would mourn.
She placed the books back on the pile and stood looking at the desolate stack.
Soon some-one would come to collect these items so forlorn, tattered and torn
So little left, to show, that she had lived on this earth so vast and wide.

In the distance she could hear the sounds of footsteps echoing on the cold, hard floor
All was quiet except for the tapping, closer and closer, finally arriving,
Stopping, clanking, and rattling the locks and doors.

The old woman turned away from the door, she didn't want to see the sympathy
On the face on the guard, as he removed her pitiful collection.
Another hour to wait before the priest would arrive with the guards.
She was ready, had been ready for the last twenty years
She wondered still why her son never came to visit.
When after all she had given him life and then had given up life for him.
Some times she did wonder what would have happened
If someone had broken her façade and found out the truth about her past
And how she had lied the day her husband died.

My Sister Noelene

Noelene never climbed mountains high,
Or swam rivers deep, nor wanted to try.
She was happy with hubby and kids of four
Never wished nor wanted for anything more.

Children now grown she has time to sit,
With patterns and wool she loves to knit.
Clicketty clack the needles sing along
Wool twisted, knitted, no stitches go wrong.

She knits as she watches the T.V shows
Little neat stitches all in patterns and rows.
Giant fluffy teddies for the grandkids dear
Warm slippers or tiny teddies to give away to cheer.

The welcome mat always rests at the door
Home neat and tidy, no mess upon the floor.
Never in a panic, ready with a smile
She makes the visit worthwhile.

Always there to listen, help or feed
She quietly goes about filling your need.
Tasty cookies and cake, she finds time to bake
Home cooked from a recipe, not a packet fake.

She never needed to climb those mountains high
But her special deeds almost reach the sky.
An angel couldn't be as sublime
As this gentle loving sister of mine.

This Is Freedom

The small child kicked and struggled,
turning his head from side to side
his little fists punching into space
he rolled over on to his belly
bringing his knees up he crawled away
and hid behind the curtains not wanting to go to bed.

In a far away land a man in tattered clothes
stood in the rain looking at the barb wire fence
his skinny body was coated in layers of mud and dirt
he raised his face to the falling rain and smiled
he may never get out from behind that fence
but at this moment in time he was free.

An old woman lying in a cold, damp nursing home bed
stares into space, while she listens for the help to come
she blanks her mind to the pictures that she doesn't want to see
wriggling a little in the dampness she loses her concentration
and the pictures come in a kaleidoscope
of times when she was young and strong and carefree.

The young woman with her baby belly
hadn't reached the due time for the bub to arrive
she had arrived at the hospital for a progress check
but then the piercing sharp pains and the baby was on the way.
No longer content to wallow inside, in it's confined space
this little bub had decided NOW was the time to break free.

A dark haired woman sitting on a bench crying
for the man who may never come home
who may be even sick or dead, killed in a senseless war
where there are no winners amongst the poor,

all signs of hope almost gone leaving just sorrow and anguish
amongst the few left behind by the cruel rebel army.

From the open church door hymns were being sung
by beautiful voices in perfect harmony
they were singing about a Lord up high
who would come and set free all the sinners by and by
But if he doesn't come soon and help us all
who amongst us will be still be here to be set free?

I Knew Her Once

She was the girl on the edge of a group
she smiled when others made fun of her
her clothes were last years fashions
she picked up others mess, carelessly left behind
we called her Sadie, I never knew her real name.

She comforted if a child fell and skinned their knees
she shared her meagre lunch with those who had none
she only just passed exams, never top of the class
she was never included in class plays
nor ever asked to a sleep over or birthday parties.

You're telling me she made world wide news
that she became a missionary
that she became a legend in a far away country
that she gave her life to save another
unselfishly putting herself in danger
Yes I knew her once, but it seems not at all.

Oh, Why....

Why would you want to,

Stick a needle in your arm, and do lots of harm?

Why would you want to,

Smoke that awful weed, when you really need a good feed?

Why would you want to,

Swallow a little pill, when it could make you ill, or kill?

Why would you want to,

Cut yourself about, making you bleed, when to death that will lead?

Why would you want to,

Take a rope and twist it tight, just to end a little fight?

Why would you want to,

Take a gun and fire it, making yourself the target to hit?

Why would you want to,

Jump from something high, when you know you can't fly?

Why would you want to,

Put you foot to the floor, when a crash impact will make you sore?

Why would you want to,

Hurt me this way, and make my days all grey?

TELL, me Why would you want to,

Kill yourself, when I would miss you so,

NO I don't want you to go! Just tell me,

We can work it out, BUT not if you are not about.

Please Just TELL me, Nothing is as bad as it seems,

]Let's make some other dreams.

Why would you want to,

Because you are loved you know,We need you to stay, not go.

Mary's Life

Mary struggled to keep her feet from slipping in the mud,
Her calloused hands clutched heavily laden pails of fodder.
Damp hair hung forward across tired eyes
She would love to rest her weary back
But knew the jobs were unfinished as yet,
Still the cow to milk, chickens to feed, and eggs to collect.

As she trudged towards the barn she thought of her sisters
At their jobs in the city so far away.
They had packed and left as soon as Mother had allowed.
From the few letters received it seemed neither had found
The life or luxuries they had craved.
One worked in a guest house, the other was a nanny,
Both worked long thankless hours for little pay.

Brother Jim had lost his life in a far away land
Fighting a war he did not understand.
Father had died long ago from over work,
Heavy drinking and hate of the family farm.
Last year Mother had finally lost the battle
Against an illness so long and cruel.

Mary stopped at the fence around the barn
And smiled as she looked out over the land.
Through the misty rain she could see
Pastures of green, where the cattle grazed.
Rock heaps in the mud, fences of strong wire
Water troughs and weathered paling sheds.
Tall timbers on the distant hills, still scared
With brown patches where years ago a fire had raged.

Mary loved the farm and the life,
The feeling of achievement when all the work was done.
Winter would soon be over until next year,
Spring lambs would start frolicking and bleating.
Trees would burst into blossom and making a cheery picture,
Pretty flowers with their perfume wafting on a gentle breeze.

The summer with the constant heat and flies,
The vegies so fresh and crisp to eat and freeze,
The plentiful fruit to bottle or make into sweet jams.
Hay to be cut, workers to feed,
Meat to salt and make into ham,
The constant worry about water, fire and drought.

Mary also loved being John's wife,
She loved to snuggle into his warm sleeping body
On cold, dreary winter nights and dream,
Thoughts of summer in winter
To pretend all the bills were paid....
To picture her unborn child at play,
As she herself had played on the same farm.
This was her heritage, her life
She would neither change nor wish to change anything.

Fire

Wind strong and relentless, blowing leaves and dust
Fanning the bushfire in the hills
Overhead is a chopper towing a water bag
That swings about in the unforgiving wind
As the pilot tries to drop water over the flames.

Night and day the wind blows, chopping and changing
First towards homes then, back to the bush.
A huge smoke haze fills the sky, hiding the hot sun
Smoke and wind slides into homes through tiny cracks
Filling homes with burnt stench that lingers on.

Tired and weary firemen in their heavy protective suits
No longer look for rain
They just plod along doing their job.
Their faces black with soot and sweat
Drink warm sweet tea, and eat with dirty hands
Then turn back to the wilderness of heat and smoke.

Homes left vacant are an easy target
For the low life thieves who show no respect.
They sneak in and steal to sell for drugs and drink.
Just what sort of evil man could light a fire?
Then wait to see the damage it causes.
These types of evil men should be given a hand full of hot coals
And let them feel the pain from fire and heat.

Bush animals try to out run the heat of flames
Some succeed others don't make it.
Birds too, fall victims as the smoke confuses them,
They no longer know which way to safety
Their cries for help go unheard in the crackling of the fire,

They fall perishing in the hot embers.

The rain has come at last but much too late
Many acres of vegetation and wild life are lost,
Along with homes, sheds and fences.
Huge tall and proud trees once stood
Some with eagles giant nests high above the earth
Now no leaves, just trunks glistening now in the soft rain
Instead of grass just a carpet of grey ashes.

Christmas Time

The bees are busily buzzing on the flowers
The weather has warmed up at last
The blow flies are arriving noisily
To sit on exposed flesh and food
Lilies are blooming with frosty white petals
Christmas is coming, Yes Christmas is coming.

Homes and businesses are all decked out brightly
There are trees with tinsel and flashing lights
Presents are being wrapped and popped under the tree
Shops are selling all fancy cakes and treats
Christmas carols can be heard on the radio
And in many stores, or sung by a choir at church.

Yes Christmas is coming, Christmas is coming
Whether you believe or not in the Holy Book
Christmas is the time of year to believe
In the miracle of love and giving
Yes Christmas is coming, Christmas is coming.

Morning Walk

Out for a walk over the hills I found it one day;
A small brook passing through pastures of green,
Twisting and turning with the fall of the land.
The clear water bubbling and gurgling,
Cascading gently between a bed of rocks,
Made smooth and polished,
From the constant flow over thousands of years.

On quiet pools the sun reflected the soft blue sky,
While on the ripples it made rainbow hues,
Glinting and sparkling before mixing with the flow.
In a nearby tree birds chirped their merry song,
Not disturbed by my presence.

In the distance a tractor engine chugging away,
Belching fumes from the exhaust; polluting
Both the air and the serenity of the early winter morning.
Loud mooing from the cattle now as they realized,
Their breakfast of hay was on the tractor tray.
Bees had now started to buzz by,
Busily fluttering from flower to flower.
My tranquil walk at an end, I turned and retraced,
My footsteps still imprinted in the morning dew.

I am Me

I have tried to fit in, so hard,
It isn't easy. I look different, speak slow.
My hair isn't cut all trendy.
My unhappiness I try not to show.
You and your friends point at me
Then double in silly giggles so loud.
Sometimes one of you will pretend,
To be nice and friendly,
Bring me over to the group,
Then just put me down in the end.

I know I shouldn't cry over this at all.
I should try to walk my own path,
Learn not to depend on friends.
I try to study hard, but at school I hear
Those sniggers that cut me in half.
I am young and haven't yet worked out
That by far I am a better person than you,
I don't need to hurt anybody at all,
I would rather help than hurt.
I just wish I was strong enough to stand tall.

I am not bright at the lessons at school,
But I listen and try my best to learn,
But I am not a complete fool.
I am not a raving beauty, my parents not rich,
I dress in the best my family can afford.
I have goals and dreams
They may not as high as some
They may never come true,
But they are my goals and my dreams.

I am ME, most of the time I get by,
But will you, as the years go by suffer,
When you realize the pain you caused,
When you haven't got those friends for a buffer,
When those friends of yours are no longer there
Will you then feel left out and alone,
Will you then, remember me?

A thought about bullying in schools of today

Waiting

I hate waiting, I am not good at it at all!

If I am at home it is okay
I can continue with the work of the day
If I am at the Doctors, I get restless
Especially when I'm sick and in stress.
Other people coughing, sniffing, comparing
Some just sitting and staring.
If I wasn't real sick when I went in
You can be sure I'll catch somethin'.

When I am at the bank in line...
I wish sometimes the bank was Mine.
I would sack the staff, and employ
Some useless street girl or boy.
They could do no worse, I'm sure
They would soon have people out the door.

Waiting at the supermarket in an endless queue
When there is a check-out staff of two
No, matter what time of day I go
It is always the same problem you know.
No staff, sorry just sold out,
Just want us to come again, no doubt.

When I ring some business I'm told to 'hold'
They don't care if I'm at the phone box getting cold
Then it's 'ring back later, he is out to lunch'
He just is hiding I've got a sneaky hunch.
The cheque is in the mail, last week he said
That's okay, I have no money even for bread.

Waiting is an art that I do not wish to learn
I have much better ways, my time to burn.
I can go for long walks to a mountain or the sea,
I can fritter my hours away on Me...
I can cook, get a book to read, or sew
I can even sneak off to a movie show.
No if I have to give to something a miss
Waiting will be on the top of the list.

Labels

We live in a modern society
Where it has now became a damned necessity
Of being what is classed as Politically correct.
I wrote a story. On the computer I did select
'Spelling/ Gramma'. Never again will I do
What that stupid program told me that I had to.
Woman now had to become Human
Which left me really fumin'.
Sexist we must no longer be
When I show you, you will see.

The frantic woman grabbed my arm..
Became 'the frantic human'..... Stay calm.
Am I now an animal I ask you,
What would you blinkin' do?
When the machine is coded with rubbish like that
It would make you want to eat your hat.

When advertising a job, one must never write
Male or female. Why not, I'd like someone to enlight.
Surely the choice should be mine,
If I'm paying the wages for working time.
Surely in this enlightened age we know if we have the skill
To fulfil the job of a Jack or a Jill.

And those labels Mrs. Ms or Missy.
These to me are as rude as can be.
Why does a female her married status have to declare
When men never have to share
So, to me, to be politically correct
We should never select.
We should just be Man, Woman, Girl or Boy,
Now I'll have another go at that computer toy.

Oh, For Solitude

Oh, for solitude, for quiet, for peace
Where movement is at a cease,
Where my thoughts are just my own,
Where I can remember the seeds that I have sown.

Not for like today, people at the door,
Their rubbish all over the floor.
Food to prepare, drinks to make, washing up to do,
Noise, loud voices, but some laughter too.

Oh, I long quiet, no junk in sight.
Well are you listening to my plight?
Will you come again, and break my peace?
You, those kids and the dog that is off its leash.

Or do you realize that I really do like to see
My grand child and sit him on my knee,
To have him cuddle in close and tight,
Squeezing me with all his might.

But I also need to have this quiet time,
Do you understand these needs of mine?
I hope you do, 'cause although I like to see you go,
I also like to see you come back, to visit, you know.

TASSIE...

This is where I want to be,
On this island of diversity.
Today it's sunny and warm,
Tomorrow it will be frost at dawn.
Yesterday I remember well,
I thought the wind was from Hell.
People to visit, places to see,
Most of it all for free.
Rich farms wide rivers, mountains tall
Yes, to me Tassie has it all.
Winter brings winds, rain, hail and snow,
To the soft white clad mountains skiers go.
Summer brings the sun, heat and drought,
Then it's off to the sand and sea to laze about.
On the rare occasions that I have left,
Believe me I have felt quiet bereft.
I just can't wait to return to be
On this Island of Diversity.

The Dream

I awoke to the new day full of hope,
Although no memory of yesterday, I knew I would cope.
I somehow knew, here I'd be safe and find
Happiness with someone who had been so kind.
Venturing into the kitchen I was greeted with the glow of a smile
I sat on the chair and watched him a while,
From whence he came, or even I,
I simply have no clue, I cannot lie.
'Good morning Bee, come eat with me
A delicious treat for you' said he
Buckwheat, in a steaming butter sauce.
'It's very good for the soul' he said with slight remorse.
I sat and stared at the offering... Buckwheat
To consume any would be a mayor feat.
But the warm room relaxed me enough to try
'Sheer Ambrosia, food for gods' I said with a sigh.

I tried my predicament to clear
Of how or why I was here.
Or even who was this gentle, smiling Andrew
Any more about him I had no clue,
Or how, his name I knew.
I remember though, he had called me Bea,
It was something he had done instinctively.

Outside the sun shimmered on the sea,
So blue and smooth, unlike the turmoil inside me.
He took my hand in a gentle hold
And told me, a story he would unfold.

I pressed my fingers to his soft lips,
While my silly heart done bumps and flips.

'No my love, say nothing, keep quiet,
Let me live in perfect peace for another night'.
We walked to the cliff top and drank in the view,
We moved as one, not as two.

The Picture On The Wall

The old man smiled at the picture on the wall
The girl standing so slim, proud and tall
Eyes of molten brown, hair hanging so silky and sleek
A healthy blush upon her smooth young cheeks
A small pup and child playing at her feet,
A book forgotten on the garden seat.
The rocking chair creaks and groans
As the old man rocks with a steady drone
He sees the girl, the babe, the dog at play
And remembers like it was yesterday.
So happy and full of life
His son and beautiful young wife.

The years once so happy, now unkind
After 90 years he is almost blind
His speech now slurred, his movements so painfully slow
Soon he knows he will be allowed to go
To where his love waits at the Pearly Gates
He has been ready for forty years, so he wont be late.
When tragedy took his son and wife
He lost interest in love, laughter and life
He gently rocks, dreams and sleeps
He knows no-one at his passing will weep,
No one left, no memories to share and recall
The picture is just a picture to others after all.

Just A Dog

If I have heard it once, it is a million times
IT IS JUST a DOG
It is not just-a-dog,
It's a companion, company, a focus,
A trusted family member,
Some reason to keep on living.

Buying the food, bath time and looking for fleas
Watching his eyes roll as I fondle his ears,
Receiving a loving lick in return.
Listening to him yelp in his dreams
He relies on me, as I rely on him.

I can tell Just-a-dog all my secrets
Knowing that they will be kept.
Just-a-dog is company on my morning walks,
Or at the sandy beach, and jumping at waves,
Shaking his body and showering water drops.

Just-a-dog knows which company I prefer,
Plus, he knows the ones not to be trusted.
The car is Just-a-dogs prize possession,
Sitting on the front passenger seat,
Guarding the car when he is left in it alone.

Just-a-dog has places in many people's hearts.
We try to protect them from everything,
When things so wrong and sickness comes
We suffer and suffer, for days, weeks or years
Just-a-dog was not just a dog, but family to me.

Printed in the United States
By Bookmasters